This book
belongs to

# Gigi, Look!

By Jo Ann Warren

**Author:** Jo Ann Warren
**Designer:** Jennifer Tipton Cappoen
**Editor:** Lynn Bemer Coble
**Photo Credit for photo of Jo Ann Warren and her grandson on the stage:** Dagmar Dankova from Dagmar Photography

**PCKids** is an imprint of **Paws and Claws Publishing, LLC.**
1589 Skeet Club Road, Suite 102 #175
High Point, NC 27265
www.PawsandClawsPublishing.com
info@pawsandclawspublishing.com

ISBN # 978-1-946198-19-8
Printed in the United States

## Acknowledgements

It is with heartfelt thanks that I acknowledge my dear children, family, and friends for their never-ending, loving support. My sincere appreciation to Lynn and Jennifer at Paws and Claws Publishing, LLC. I especially want to thank Cindy Hollingsworth for her encouragement, advice, and inspiration.

## Dedication

For Bill.

"Come on, Gigi.
Time to go out and about.
Time to see what we can see."

"Wait. Wait!"

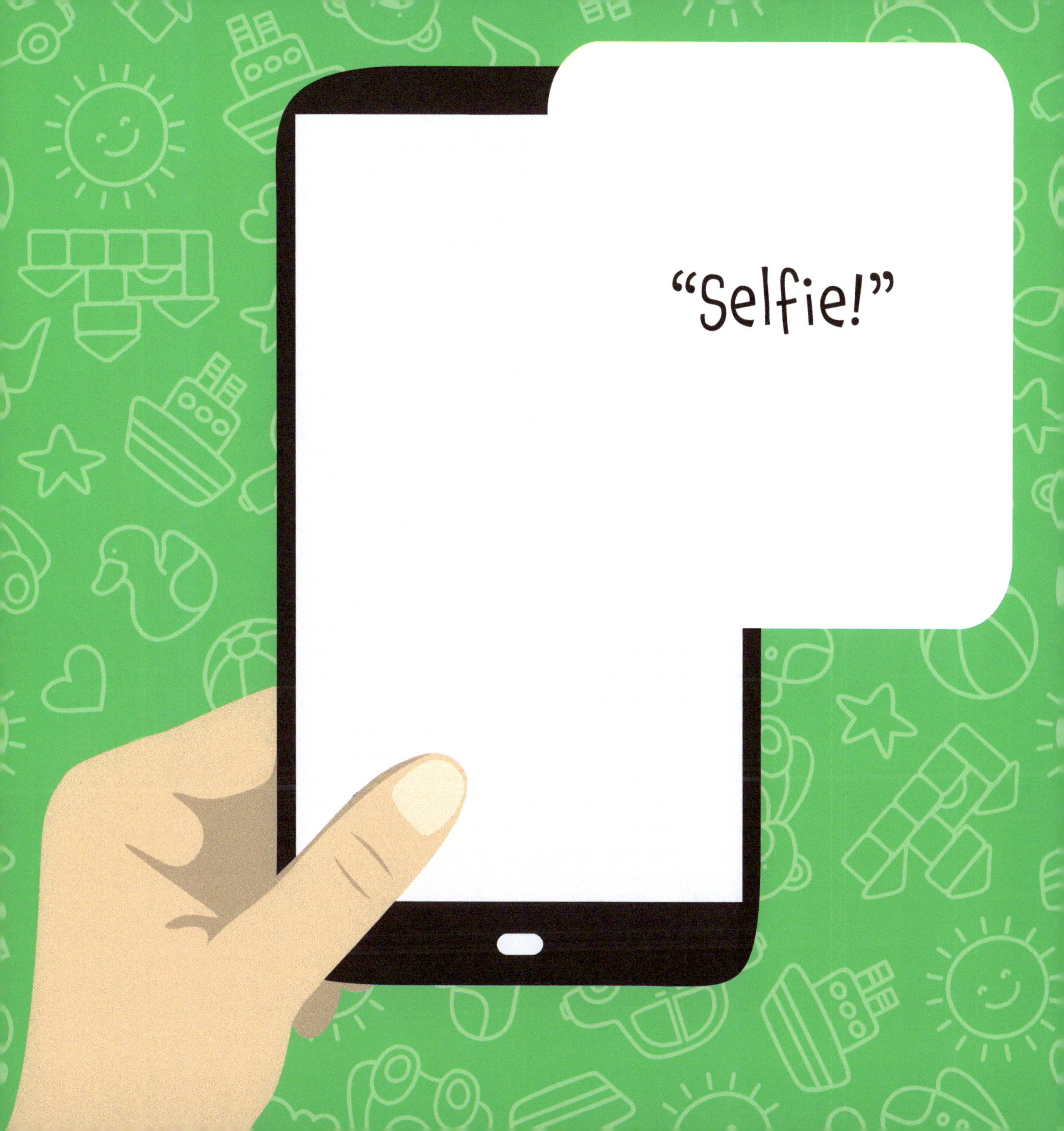
"Selfie!"

"Oh, Gigi, we look silly."

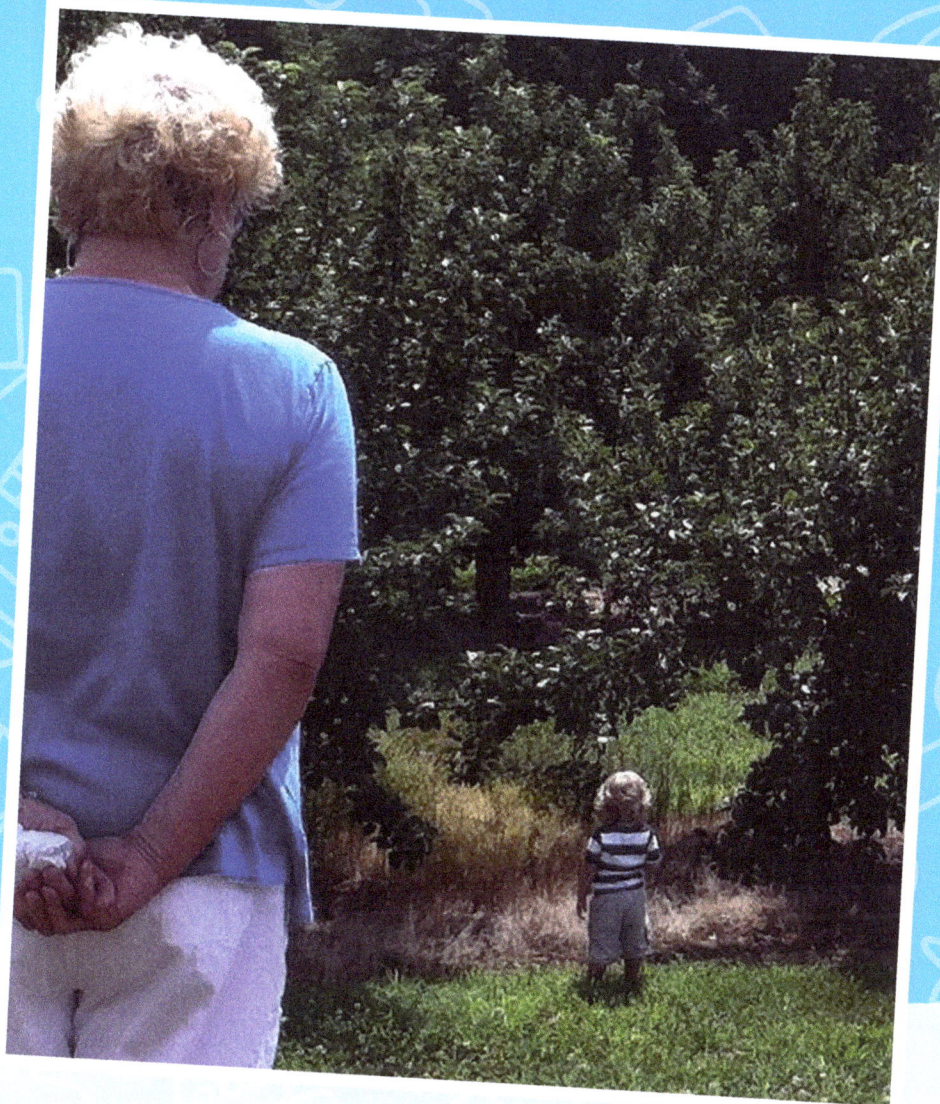

"Gigi, look! See the trees.
See the apples."

"Apples.
Apple juice.
Applesauce.
Apple slices!"

"We are at the orchard!"

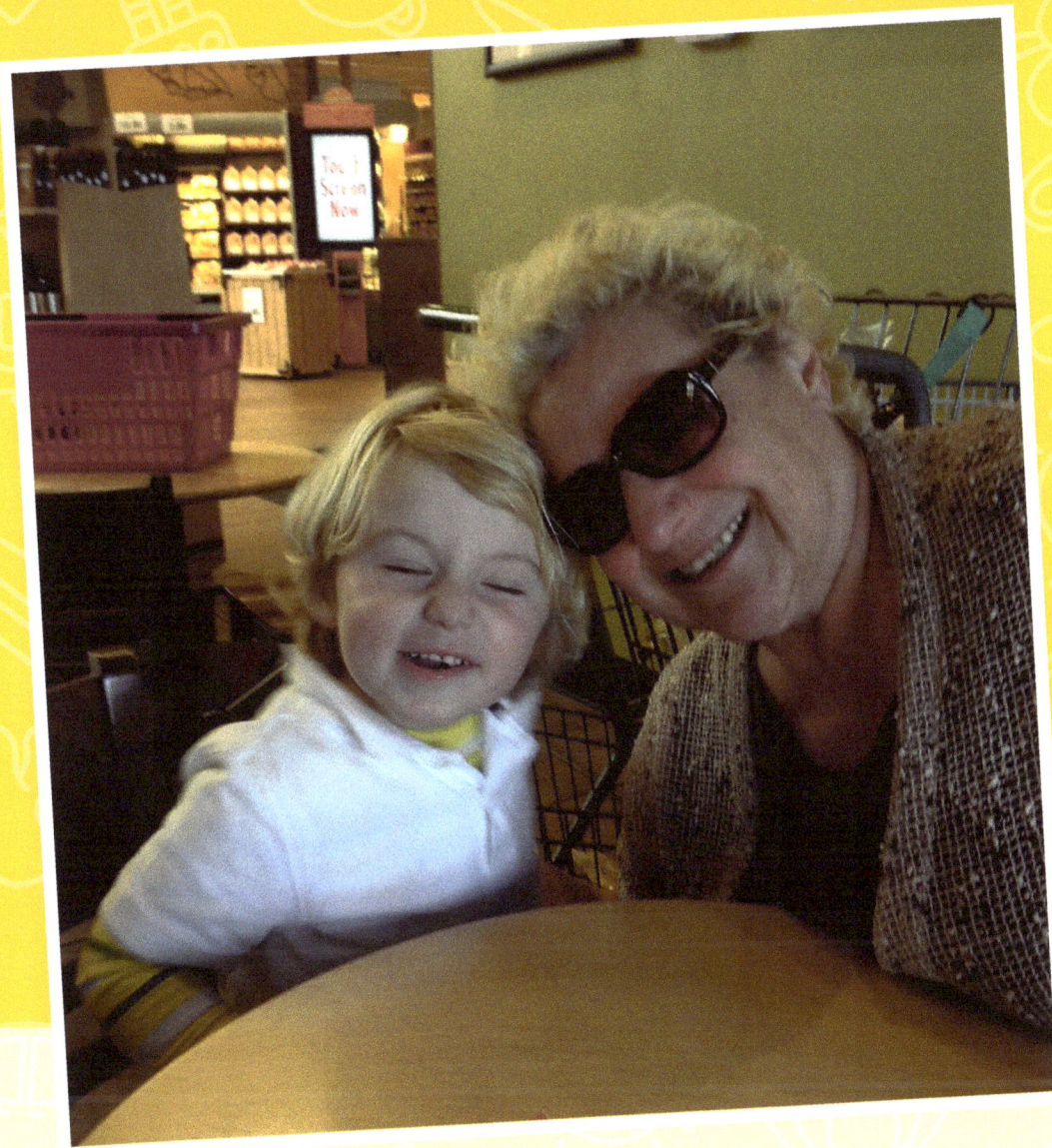

"Gigi, look! See the food. See the cart."

"We are at the market.
I love shopping!"

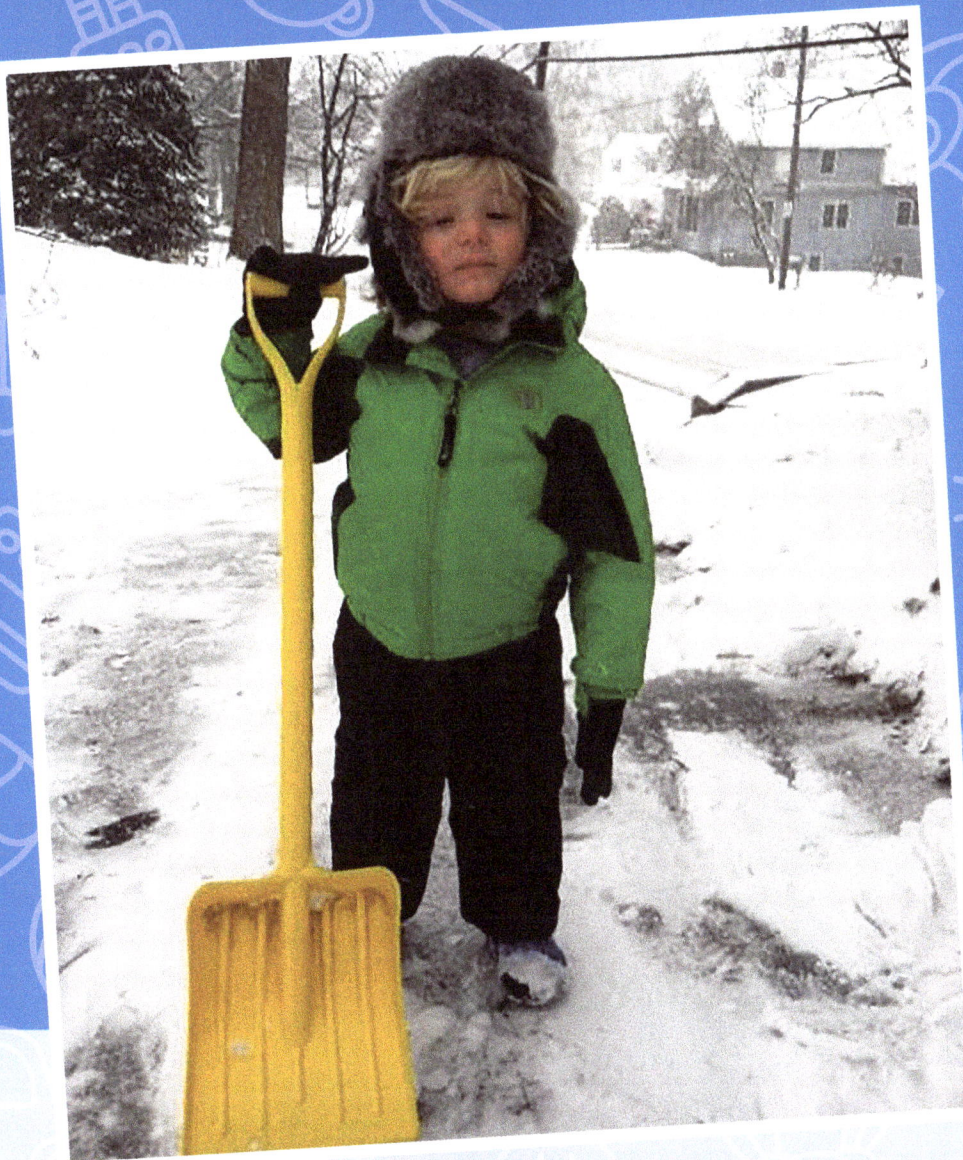

"Gigi, look! See my shovel.
See the snow."

"Guess who is coming.
You know."

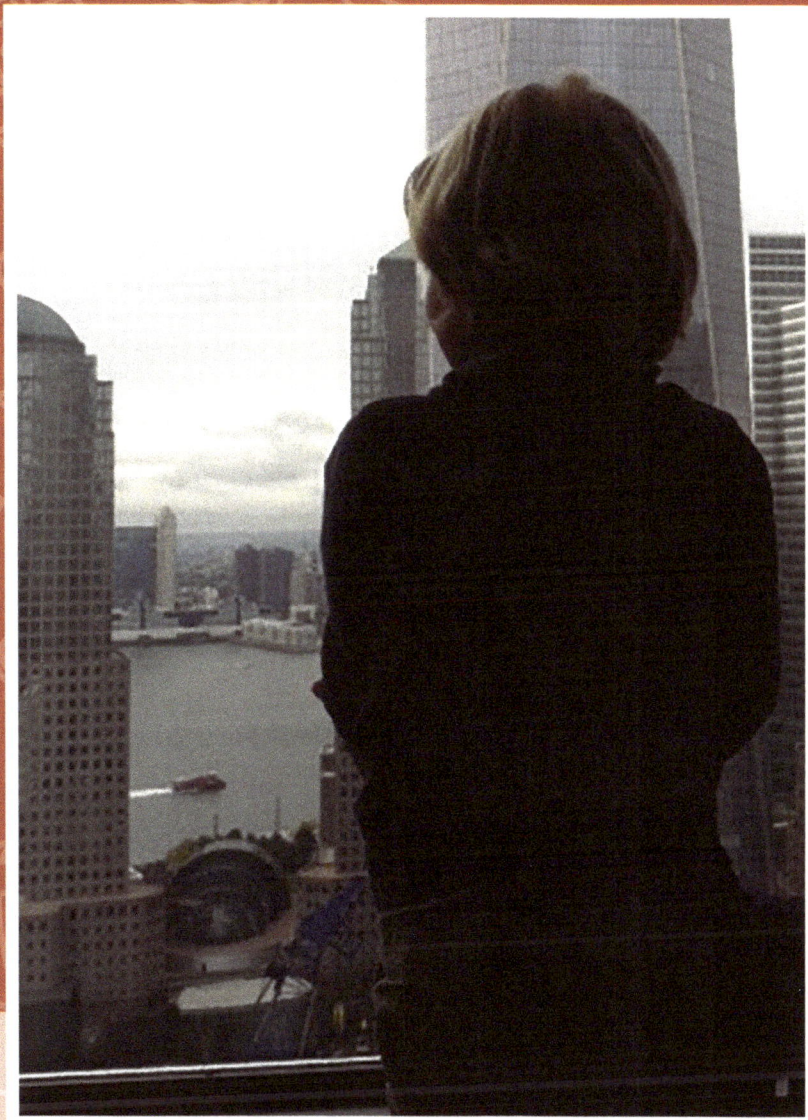

"Gigi, look! See the tall buildings.
See the small boat."

"We are in the city.
Gigi, we can rest and watch here."

"Gigi, look! See the water.
See the tube."

"We are in the pool.
This is you and me, Gigi."

"Gigi, look! See the table.
See the chair."

"We are at the restaurant.
Gigi, I am not good at waiting."

"Gigi, look! See the stage.
See the curtain."

"We are at the show. Watch me dance. Gigi, watch me. Watch me."

"Gigi, look! See the baby chick.
See the sun. This is new."

"Gigi, look! See the cows.
See the sheep."

"We are at the farm. The dairy farm! Vanilla with rainbow sprinkles, please."

"Gigi, look! See the kids.
See the hoop."

"We are at the park.
Yippee!"

"Gigi, look! See the people.
See all the people. We are at..."

"Gigi. Gigi."

"Gigi! Gigi!"

"There you are, Gigi. I see you."

"Gigi, look! See the water.
See the ducks."

"We are at the lake.
Pedal, Gigi. Pedal."

"Gigi, look! See the blocks.
See the castle."

"We are at the museum.
I am looking for the princess."

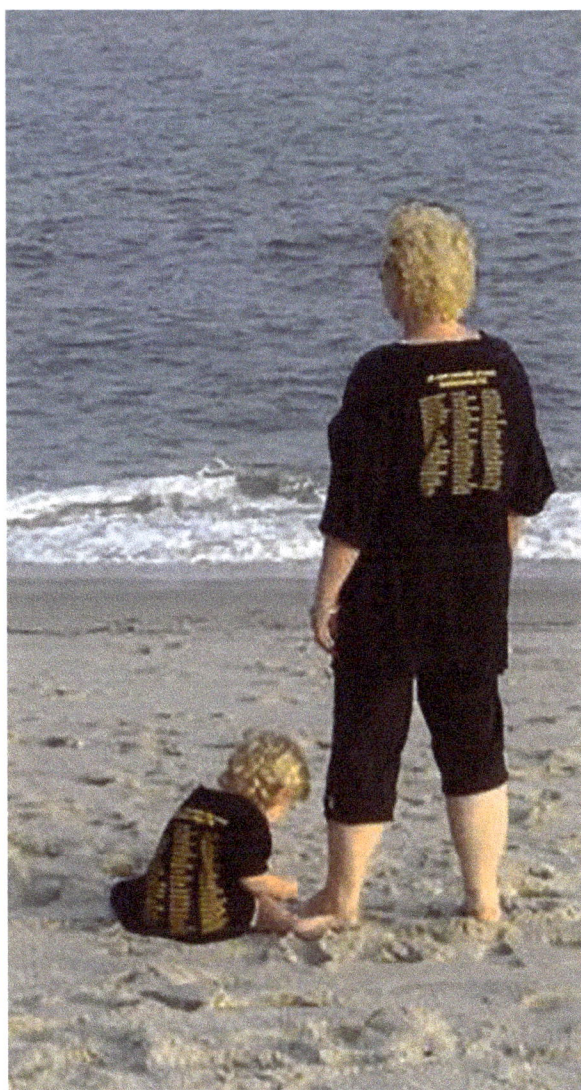

"Gigi, look! See the ocean.
See the waves."

"We are on the shore.
What a good day!"

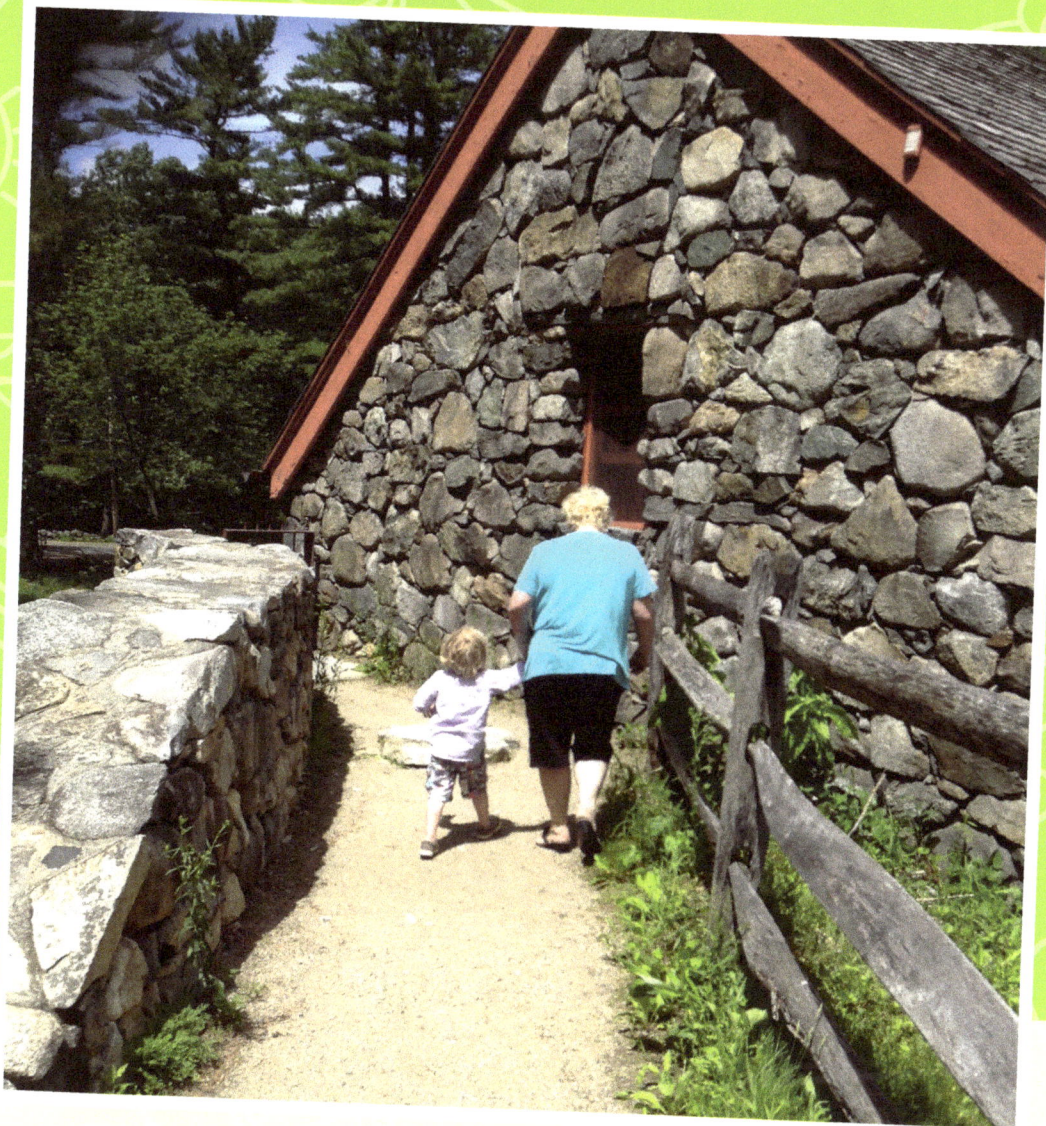

"Gigi, look! See all the rocks.
See the fence."

"We are at an old mill.
Old. Old. Very old."

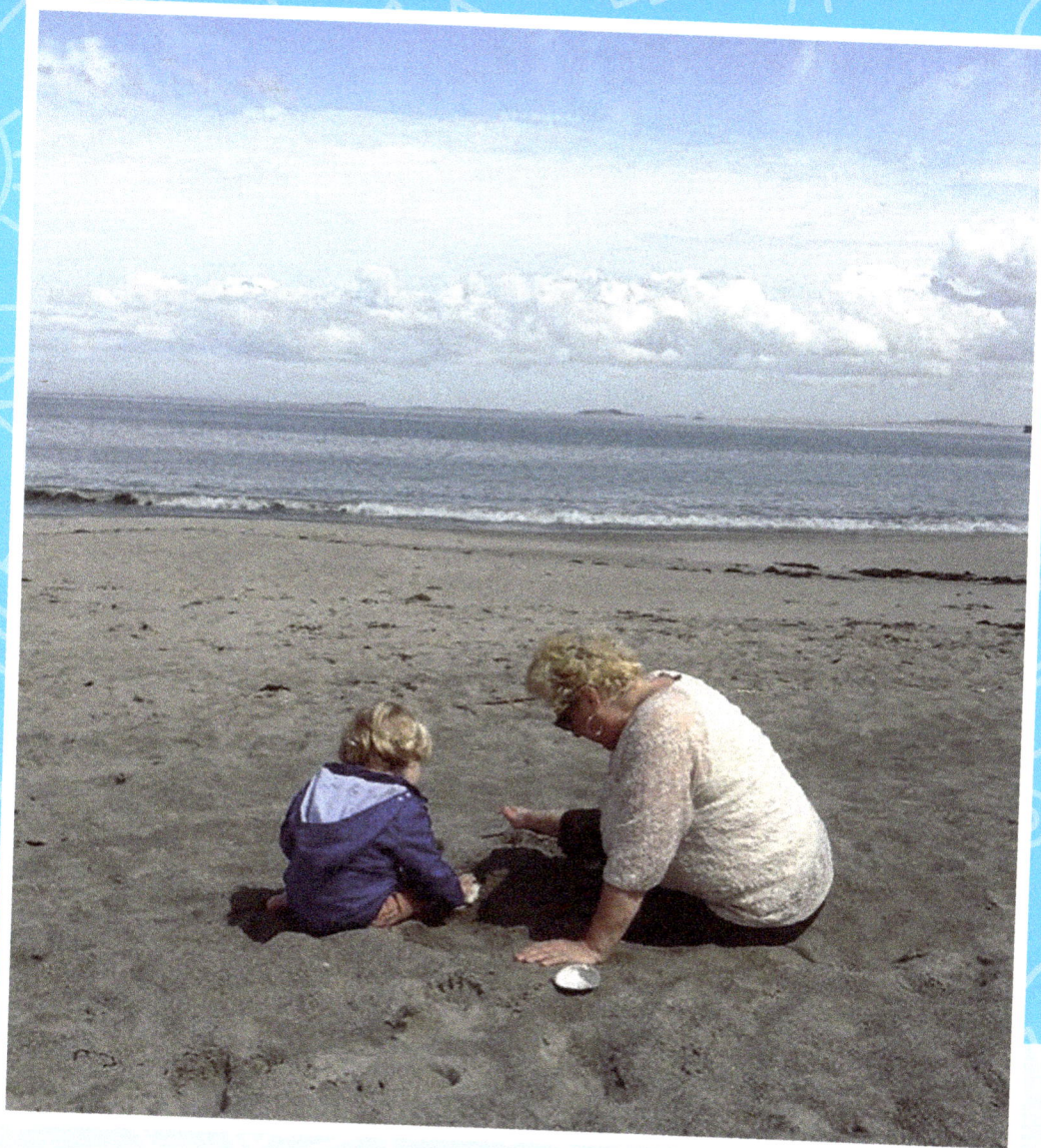

"Gigi, look! See the shells.
See the sand."

"We are at the beach. Look.
I found a friend, Gigi."

"Gigi, look! See the band.
Hear the music."

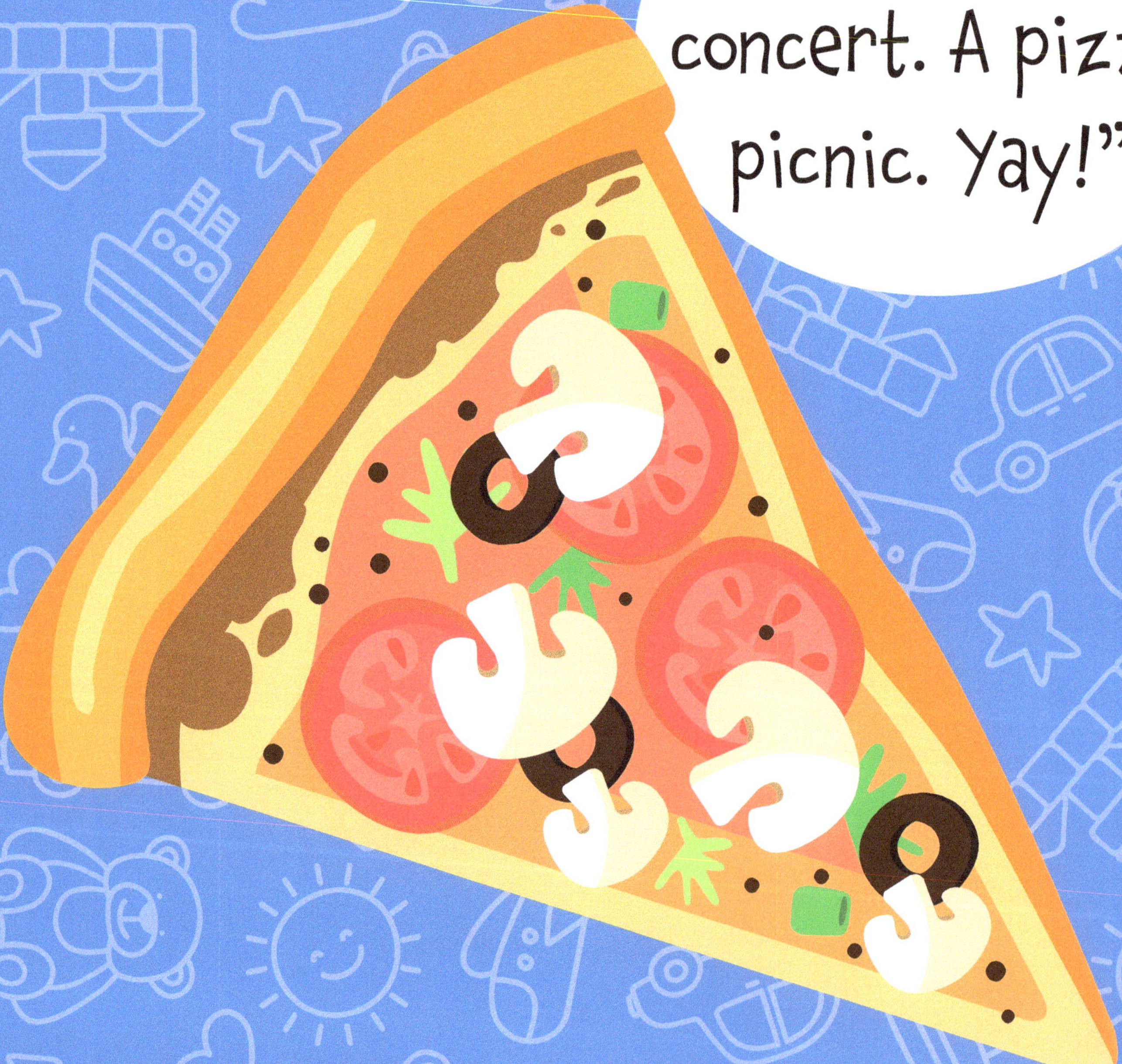

"We are at the concert. A pizza picnic. Yay!"

"Gigi, look! See my sandbox.
See my little toys. We are in the yard."

" Look closely, Gigi. Fall is coming around again."

"If we look, we can

see everything!"

## About the Author

Author Jo Ann Warren battles with severe blepharospasm. This is a diagnosed condition with no known cause and no cure. It affects both her vision and the quality of her life. After five years of uncertainty and darkness, her condition is under control thanks to Dr. Nutan Sharma.

In this book, Jo Ann allows readers to see the world through her grandson's beautiful young eyes and kind loving heart.

Jo Ann is the proud owner and director of Jo Ann Warren Studio, a Massachusetts performing-arts school established in 1979. It is well known for a tradition of excellence.

She spends every minute possible living life to the fullest and making more memories with her grandson.

www.ingramcontent.com/pod-product-compliance
Lightning Source LLC
LaVergne TN
LVHW070841080426
835513LV00024B/2427